DAILY THOUGHTS FOR THE ADVENT JOURNEY

He will be gracious to you as you journey.
He will hear your cry.
When he hears, he will answer.

When the Lord has given you the bread of suffering
and the water of distress,
he who is your teacher will hide no longer
and you will see him with your own eyes.

When you turn to right or to left on your journey
your ears will hear these words behind you:
'This is the way, follow it.'
Isaiah 30:19-21

Niall Ahern

Daily thoughts for the Advent Journey

the columba press

First published in 2010 by
the columba press
55A Spruce Avenue, Stillorgan Industrial Park,
Blackrock, Co Dublin

Designed by Bill Bolger

The cover picture is The Flight into Egypt, sculpture from
North West Transept, Cathedral of the Immaculate Conception,
Sligo.
The illustrations in this book are by Sóirle Mac Cana and are
taken from *Irish Craftmanship* (Irish Hospitals' Trust, 1940) and
are used by permission
Origination by The Columba Press
Printed in Ireland by ColourBooks Ltd, Dublin

ISBN 978-1-85607-719-4

Acknowledgements
These reflections by Niall Ahern, which have been delivered as
radio talks over the past few years, are adapted from Tom Cox's
Intercom liturgical cycle of Scripture Thoughts, which is to be
published soon. We hope this compendium will bring focus and
encouragement to all our Advent readers.

Contents

Foreword

Advent is a time of preparation. It is an important time for all who believe in the coming of Christ. It cannot go unnoticed or unheeded. The Messiah did not come without the preparatory period of Israel's history or without the preparatory responses of fidelity by Joseph and Mary. In our own day, Advent offers each one of us a time of preparation that must affect our lives. Christ will not come in his fullness to us unless we too are prepared.

By way of personal preparation for this season, I have listened to the series of Advent Radio Reflections delivered last year by Niall Ahern and am greatly helped by the conviction and urgency with which he encourages and impels us to engage with this vital opportunity to make ourselves ready at a personal level for Christ's coming. His gentle but insistent voice heralds forth the Good News in a sometimes bewildering world, and this collection of these Radio Reflections will be a real inspiration for so many who seek the deeper meaning of the Advent season.

I have heard Niall Ahern speak about God's word on many occasions. This little book reflects the energy, the compassion and the conviction which he brings to his ministry of preaching. This *Daily Thoughts for the Advent Journey*, which he has delivered on radio, incorporates all that we could ask of God at this time – and if we were to pray it for each other and for ourselves during the season we would all be much blessed.

We can all use this Advent book to inform our preparation for the coming of Christ. We can anticipate and marvel at his coming again as people have marvelled over the centuries. This time in which we live demands much of each of us, and if we set aside a little time to prepare for Christ to come and transform our lives again on Christmas morning we will be enriched and strengthened. May we travel the Advent journey well together!

Baroness Nuala O'Loan

Introduction

The Christian never wearies of listening to the story of the coming of Christ, of examining again the hints that God dropped into history before he was born of the Virgin Mary.

The story of God's coming amongst us in Christ reads like a child's game of hide and seek. In the history of our race it was man that first hid himself from God. Adam and his wife hid themselves among the trees of the garden and for centuries afterwards man wandered around seeking the hiding place of God who had left in the beauty of this world so many clues of his presence.

Suddenly while all things were quiet and the night was in the midst of its course, God changed his hiding place. He came and hid in a little country town, came and hid in a cave, came and hid in the form of a child. The game of hide and seek was over.

In word and thought, we retrace here the path of man's search for God and of God's search for man that ended in the joyful discovery of each other in the cave of Bethlehem. I thank Tom Cox for his Scripture Thoughts from *Intercom* on which these Radio Reflections are based, and hope that our efforts will combine to bring you new hope and insight on your Advent journey this year. I compliment The Columba Press for taking this timely initiative, and in the spirit of this season we pray:

When the world was dark and the city was quiet you came. You crept in beside us. And no one knew. Only the few who dared to believe that God might do something different. Will you do the same this Christmas, Jesus? Will you come into the darkness of today's world: not the friendly darkness as when sleep rescues us from tiredness, but the fearful darkness in which people have stopped believing that war will end or that food will come or that the government will change, or that the church cares? Will you come into that darkness and do something different to save your people from death and despair? Will you come into the quietness of our towns, not the friendly quietness as when lovers hold hands but the fearful silence when the phone has not rung, the letter has not come, the friendly voice no longer speaks, the doctor's face says it all?

Will you come into that darkness and do something different, not to distract, but to embrace your people? And will you come into the dark corners and the quiet places of our lives? We ask you because the fullness our lives long for depends on us being as open and vulnerable to you as you were to us, trusting human hands to hold their maker. Will you come into our lives if we open them to you, and do something different?

When the world was dark and the city was quiet, you came. You crept in beside us. Do the same this Christmas, Jesus. Do the same this Christmas.

With blessings on your Advent journey and throughout the Christmas season.

Niall Ahern

Advent Prayer

God, our Father,
through the power of the Holy Spirit,
you sent your Son,
Jesus Christ,
to come as a little child
to lead us
on our Advent journey.

As we prepare this Advent
for his coming again,
open our hearts to the wonder
of his Presence
in our lives.

Heal our wounds,
bless our endeavours,
and make us gentle of heart.

Amen

First Week

Week 1: Sunday

Today is the first Sunday of Advent: it's about starting on a journey, a new adventure.

It's how we travel that is important now, how we prepare for those we will meet at our destination.

Most of us have had the experience of absent-mindedly getting into our car, and arriving at the destination with no recollection of the journey. That is, until you have a near miss, and then you notice everything to the point of paranoia. Some things can become second nature to us, so that we become inoculated from reality. We travel on autopilot. Advent is meant to be like some great red light in your face. You stand on the brakes and take notice.

In the midst of all the hustle and bustle of Christmas time, with the Christmas shopping, with the Christmas decorating, with the Christmas parties, with the Christmas music specials and the special liturgies, we often travel through the season of Advent without paying much attention to him whom we are preparing to receive.

Why are we getting ready to throw this big party on December 25th? Why are we doing all this stuff? The birth of Jesus Christ. Nothing more, nothing less. With only four weeks to go, there's time. Maybe not for all the external things, but for what really counts – people and the person of Jesus Christ. Time enough as well to answer the question asked of the Baptist: Who are you? Why are you here?

And what are you going to do? Why are you travelling this road? And who do you hope to meet at journey's end? Make a good start today. Keep focus!

Amen.

Week 1: Monday

Today is the first workday of Advent and it's about waking up to newness.

Many people find their biological clock unerringly wakens them in time. Somehow, if you must catch the early flight or train, anything out of the normal routine, the body responds just in case you forget to set the clock.

Sometimes the world conspires against this – with the abundance of public lighting even urban birdlife can be tricked into thinking it's daytime. Humans beings are not unlike that either – they too can be tricked: with just twenty-two days left to Christmas they think today is wake-up time for shopping.

But this first Monday of Advent is a unique day, towards the end of the calendar year and at the beginning of the liturgical year. It's a Monday charged with newness as we turn our faces to the future, and yet each of us feels individually at a kind of end – it's a different wakeup call, the challenge to leave behind certain things and to start new things. It's about faith, renewal in faith. You see, if Advent is only waiting for Christmas, then what you get is just celebration and presents and carols and food. If Advent is just a journey, and Christmas the destination, then as wonderful as Christmas is, it will become only a good memory and it will always run the risk of becoming a sentimental journey with little depth.

But if Advent has a beginning and an ending, then it's a journey of faith, a trip we make into the heart of God. Advent is preparation with a beginning and an end, a preparation of our hearts for the heart of God. We are being called today to wake up to the reality that we can end certain selfishness in our lives and begin new kinds of loving.

I hope you hear that wakeup call of faith for yourself this first workday of Advent.

Amen.

Week 1: Tuesday

Advent is about ringing the changes, not just the tills.

The French may think that they discovered revolution in 1789, to be followed by changes, by movements and countries who portrayed themselves in turn as the latest revolutionaries. History has proved them all wrong.

Maybe the real revolutionary today is the Christian. Why? Because he or she is prepared to change themselves. That is the greatest change – by changing ourselves we gradually transform the world.

Advent is one of those times in the year when we especially think of this personal change. But will the notion of personal change this Advent remain just that, an idea? Have we, to quote Eliot, 'had the experience and missed the meaning'.

In terms of sacraments, is our passport all stamped on the right pages – baptised, confirmed, married, confessed – but never really an integral part of us. No more than the pharisees, a strong case of mixed motives. Just as it was for John, we have three distinct groups when it comes to God's call at Advent: those who have already given up – there's no response or possibility of change; those who heard him but whose hearts were hardened and reluctant to change; those who came to John full of hope and with a real preparedness to change.

Which of these groups do you belong to this Advent? Amen.

Week 1: Wednesday

Advent is about the unexpected.

No human being can live without hope, something to live for or look forward to, otherwise we give way to despair. This was true even for John the Baptist in prison as he prepared the way for Christ.

With our Advent journey just begun, will we find what we hope for or expect? The people of the Old Testament had the courage to hope for big things – that the desert would be turned into fertile ground, that their scattered and divided people would eventually be gathered again. Centuries apart from us, their hopes were no different from ours or from any human beings – lasting peace, food, shelter, an end to suffering, pain and misery.

But do we differ from them? Yes we do, in one way: Jesus has entered human history and revealed God as Emmanuel, 'God with us'. Yet, when we are feeling like John, maybe not physically imprisoned but within the prison of depression, a disability, a serious illness, chronic pain, a troubled marriage, a hum drum job, we too ask of God, 'Are you the one?'

No more than for John, the answer we receive may not be quite what we expect or feel we deserve. God's reply is on the lines: 'Don't worry. Everything is on target. The Kingdom of God is being built. Trust me.'

Advent will be what we expect, if only we can trust in God. Amen.

Week 1: Thursday

Advent asks us to have no fear. It's about not being afraid.

When you move house the physical move is one thing. Most people find the packing and unpacking aspect the most stressful. However, notifying your change of address to family, friends, colleagues and businesses, can be a real headache. Only junk mailers uncannily seem to find you at your new home address.

You see, put simply the celebration of Christmas is about the change of God's address. If names and addresses are important, this one, is all important, Emmanuel, God at home with us.

No more than human change of address, this move needs personal notification to be sent to everyone. No general notice will do, it's personal and unique for every person. That's why the real Advent greeting to Joseph began with, 'Do not be afraid.'

Is this possible, in a fear-provoking world that begat the Madrid bombs, the Beslan school massacre, the ongoing agony of Afghanistan and Iraq, the Burma protests?

Well, Ahas in the Old Testament would not surrender control to God. He would not trust God and he was stuck in his sphere. St Paul, on the other hand, totally surrendered to God at his conversion and he never looked back. Joseph acted immediately, without questioning, as soon as he woke up from his dream.

It really comes down to this: Do you trust God and have no fear? That's a question we all have to be at home for, whatever our address.

Are you at home for God this Advent?

Amen.

Week 1: Friday

Advent is about meeting expectations.

We're not good at recognising each other's worth, particularly in families. Those whom we see much, we seldom recognise.

If that is true, then consider what thoughts John the Baptist must have had when he heard what his own cousin Jesus was doing. Small wonder he sent messengers to enquire. You can almost sense the heartbreak of a man imprisoned, as John's plaintive question is put to Jesus, 'Are you the one who is to come? Or have we to wait for someone else?' In his heart, John perhaps had thought of someone else – but his own cousin.

The reply is to ask John to look at what is happening all around him. God can be seen to be present and at work in words and actions and in the person of Jesus. Talk about dashed hopes and shattered expectations! While we think we would have recognised Jesus without asking the question that John put to him, it's unlikely.

In over two thousand years, nothing has changed. People still come looking for Jesus, wondering, hoping, watching, looking for evidence that it is still real. Jesus is no longer here to meet them physically, as he did with the friends of the Baptist. That challenge falls to us who claim to live his life.

The only question we have to answer is, 'Are we the

ones that others will follow? Or, will they have to look for someone else?' What do we need to do this Advent to meet the fair expectations of those who come to us, looking for Jesus?

Amen.

Week 1: Saturday

Advent is about hope.

As the year turns to a close, there can be a haunting bitter-sweet feel to this month – hoping for loved ones to return, for health to return, balancing limited family budgets with unlimited expectations of children.

For some, the aspects that would make a happy Christmas are missing. Reality is always less than it might be.

This season of Advent is in tune with our feelings. Advent it a time to hope for *what is not*. Christmas, however, is a time to celebrate *what is*.

If Advent is a time to lament the fact that the kingdom has not come to its fullness, Christmas is a time to rejoice in the fact that the kingdom has been born in our midst.

If Advent is a time to lament the continuing power of darkness around us, Christmas is a time to celebrate the light of the world born in Bethlehem.

The point is this, Advent and Christmas are linked like two sides of the same coin. If Advent has been celebrated with the kind of bracing honesty that enables us to name and lament the ways in which evil and despair continue to rule, Christmas will naturally become a season of celebration of the grace of God, which is far stronger than evil and despair.

Christmas is hope realised. December is the time for

expressing the hope and strengthening the dreams that will carry us through the year.

Advent is the way we as a people express our hopes. Keep hope in your hearts this Advent.

Amen.

Second Week

Week 2: Sunday

Today is the second Sunday of Advent; it's about a journey into honesty; into what has stood us in good stead on life's journey.

Scenic routes are all very well, but ultimately we want to get to our destination as quickly as possible. Our Celtic ancestors would scratch their heads in amazement at the sight of an estimated 1.8 million Irish horseless chariots – 'cars' if your prefer – hurtling down broad paved roads. Their idea of a road was *'bó-thar'*, a track wide enough for one cow to pass by another. But, while we may be going faster and in style, where exactly are we ultimately headed? Is the light ahead the tail-light of the next traffic jam? What's it all about?

In situations like these, it can be helpful to get back to the beginning. Which is exactly what today's gospel does. We have a flashback to the start of St Mark's gospel. It's strange: there are no shepherds, no wise men, no stable, no Mary and Joseph or even baby Jesus. Nothing cuddly about this one. St Mark sticks to the message of repentance, our turning away from sin.

Advent is a time for us to be honest. Remember, Jesus came to take away our sins, not our brains. Just as the familiar road is often the best bet to lead us safely home, a good look at what has stood us in good stead in the past might bring us back to our senses and to God this Advent.

If there has been waywardness or inertia on our travels, then let us hear the Advent call and move into the deeper place within us where the Christ child wishes to be reborn.

Amen.

Week 2: Monday

Advent is about waiting for the visit of God.

Christmas comes, commercially, earlier and earlier each year. In a devotional sense, it only comes onto our horizon at the beginning of Advent.

It is a belated preparation for the visit of God, perhaps. Indeed, visiting family, friends and neighbours is probably a less practised art in today's world, where we surf the World Wide Web but we still don't know who lives next door. Still, for any expected visit there is preparation. A quick wipe, hoover and clean and all is ready.

But it seems a bit strange that we should begin preparing for Christ's birth and a new church year by just waiting for the visit. Almost quietly. With quiet hearts.

The secular message is to be alert and busy, but the deeper message is to wait. And it's hard. After all, leaders of any groups will admit that waiting is the biggest enemy in keeping a group of people focused and alert for the impending task. With the best will, attention and standards will fall.

Over the coming weeks, we carry out time honoured traditions, customs that link us with our past and our future and reinforce our family's personality.

Many other voices, not least of children, will remind us that we have not done something yet. But today, we listen to the divine voice telling us not to lose sight of what is ultimately important. It's an Advent attitude. A quiet attitude. God is going to visit.

Let us be quiet, lest we miss the moment.

Amen.

Week 2: Tuesday

Advent is about waiting in hope.

Nobody likes the critical person. Someone who has the negative view or word or barb – who, if it is a sunny day, will tell you that rain is coming tomorrow.

As the thronged shops operate to the joyful sound of Christmas jingles, we have in the gospel nations in agony, men dying of fear, the powers of the heavens shaken, or so the gospel says.

Pretty it isn't. But it's real. The sad truth is that all of us who are old enough know that we do not live in a Santa Claus world. Children's visions are washed away with the hot tears of grown-up disappointment and despair.

The gospel vividly shows the world ending but most people find their worlds ending in a more personal way.

A relationship ends, a loved one dies, illness intervenes, an addiction comes into the family.

When your life is rocked to its foundations, does the misery of disappointment, disease and death have the last word?

No, it doesn't. God does. What we should do is increase in love, stand erect, don't flee situations or block them out. God is at work.

Advent is more than just waiting for the Christ child, it's anticipation.

Waiting combined with hope. The hope that is sure that Christ will come to you this Advent time.

Amen.

Week 2: Wednesday

Advent is about pockets of darkness.

At a time when daylight is precious and in short supply, with darkness all around us, we celebrate the light and hope of Advent.

There are many pockets of darkness in our lives that no amount of Advent candles can dispel. And so we ponder the darkness in the heart of the man or woman who faces a future of unemployment and emigration.

The darkness in the heart of the old person whose short years are fast passing away.

The darkness in the heart of the young person who is crushed at the discovery of an unexpected pregnancy.

The darkness in the heart of the embezzler and the housebreaker.

The darkness in the heart of the adult whose illness has been pronounced terminal.

The darkness in the heart of the lonely and the wounded.

The darkness in the heart of the woman who has discovered her husband's infidelity.

The darkness in the heart of the husband whose wife's love is slipping away from him.

The darkness in the heart of an innocent captive held for ransom by a dangerous criminal.

The darkness in the heart of the dangerous criminal who will mutilate for money.

The darkness in the heart of the sick and the weak, the suffering and the bereaved, the poor and the unwanted.

Into that darkness we pray, with our Advent cry, that the Lord will come with light and healing. *Maranatha*. Come, Lord Jesus. Bring us light. Scatter our pockets of darkness this Advent time.

Amen.

Week 2: Thursday

Advent is about giving right of way to God.

The old definition of a road was where cattle could safely pass each other. Hence the word for road, *bóthar*. Thankfully communications have improved since that time.

Whatever about ease of contact today, with better roads, phones, faxes and even e-mails, God has a harder time getting through the mountains of advertising, and hills of sound are even higher than that, and the winding ways of supermarkets are slow to straighten.

Often people complain that God seems absent in their lives or that they experience nothing in prayer because God seems remote, uncaring, indifferent. Maybe we should change our perspective a bit and ask, 'What is blocking God's path? What is on the roadway?'

Sometimes we think that God chooses to be distant. But the deeper truth may be that there is something in me which makes me less accessible to God. God's absence can be the result of our fear, our resistance to change, our desire to be in control, our cynicism, our inability to love. As Christians, we might be *in* the way, not *on* the way.

Even the birthday of the Prince of Peace has become the most stressful and unhealthy time of the year.

Maybe we would all do well to spend a minute before we begin each day, wondering, 'Why am I allowing myself to become part of this stress? What's it all about?'

All the better if you ask yourself, 'Who is it about? Who is it for? Where does it lead?' We know in our hearts it leads to God.

Give God right of way this Advent.

Amen.

Week 2: Friday

Advent is about when the unexpected happens.

By now, except for some finer details, our Christmas preparations are speeding along. This checked, the perfect gift obtained and wrapped, cards delivered in time. Menus are in their final stages. The final scoot around the house, a cleaning frenzy and everything will be just right.

But we know that other things can and will happen. As one writer put it: life is something that happens to us when we are busy planning for it.

What happens when we are confronted with things that are beyond our control?

Mary had her own plans. Pregnancy and human accusations of infidelity and pleas of innocence were not part of them. Joseph didn't plan to feel isolated and lost. Not able to understand the situation Mary described. If ever a reassuring angel was needed, it was then and now.

Familiarity has dulled the drama of this gospel scene. Misunderstandings, false assumptions, fear and disappointment have their place in the jigsaw puzzle of our lives. Not the perfect situation for the Messiah to be born into, but it was the right one.

And it is the right one.

For, you see, God only wants a little room. A heart prepared to trust even the unknown, the unplanned, the unexpected.

God is Emmanuel. God is with us. Let God be the unexpected happening in your life this Advent.

Amen.

Week 2: Saturday

Advent is *about* homecoming and Christmas *is* home-coming.

Our homes and fridges are never fuller. In preceding days, airports, train stations and ferry terminals strain to cope with the extra traffic. Whatever the reality, to be away from home leads to a special home sickness and loneliness.

Many years ago, a young couple was forced by their government to spend Christmas many miles from their Nazareth home. No creature comforts, no accommodation save a stable. Yet it is here among strangers that Jesus was born.

God chose to make an entrance into our world, not in the midst of a large family gathering, but in a place no one expected – under harsh conditions in a poor region of the world.

Many people will be without a home this year. Or perhaps at home but separated from family members by death, divorce or some other unhappy circumstance. Some will spend Christmas in hospital or prison. Others will find themselves a continent away.

Wherever we are this Christmas time, whether or not joy comes easily, we need to remember that Christmas is more than party going and gift giving and receiving. It is Jesus coming to make his home in our hearts and warming our lives by his presence.

Let every heart a manger be. Let our hearts come home this Christmas.

Amen.

Third Week

Week 3: Sunday

Today is the Third Sunday of Advent: it's about an absence of a presence.

Passing by a school we attended in the past always brings back memories. The years fall away, the corridors of memory are prowled. There is a part of us forever a child. One common school experience was when a teacher left the room. They departed, leaving work to do and words of admonition. All too often the result was that one or two stood sentry, listening for the teacher's return, while the rest made mayhem or worked at the assigned task.

Switch to the gospel and the not unfamiliar sight of an absentee landlord. No more than school, some of us are childish when it comes to what the gospel asks of us. Absence is a test. Will we faithfully do the work we have been left to do? Or will we play up, hoping that we won't get caught out if he comes back unexpectedly?

It's strange how we are destined for eternity, and yet we don't know how to profitably spend the time we do have in our earthly lives. Are we letting the significant things of life sweep by us unnoticed, or are we standing on tiptoes, waiting and working at what we have been given to do and to mind?

Time never seems to work for us; it either goes too fast – with conflicting demands and pressures – or too slow so that we become lethargic and assume that nothing ever changes. Advent is a time to wake up if we have fallen alseep. After all, absence is the test!

Amen.

Week 3: Monday

Advent is about putting Herod back in Christmas.

For many people, December represents an obstacle course of tasks to undertake, things to do. It is largely a sentimental moment. Maybe we need to bring Herod back. After all, he was there at the first Christmas. He reminds us that Jesus didn't enter a world of sparkly Christmas cards or a world of warm spiritual sentiment. Jesus entered a world of real pain, of serious dysfunction, a world of brokenness and political oppression.

We come like children with a huge Christmas list, asking for all the gifts that we need. For the gifts of peace, understanding and love. We pray for

- the frustrated whose dreams lie in ruins
- the deeply ashamed who cannot forgive themselves
- the haughty who need to look again at themselves
- the overly busy who 'hide' among the clutter of incompleted tasks
- the vain who try to make an impression to fill their own emptiness
- the corrupt and morally decayed who crush and plunder other lives
- the fearful, the confused, those who are wracked with guilt or pain
- the secret hurts we won't let anyone else know about

   – the people of the world, suffering with the effects of
     war and poverty.

Herod reminds us that we live in an unequal world
where dominance may attempt to reign. Advent reminds
us that we live in the real world where Christ will come and
reign, forever and ever.

   Amen.

Week 3: Tuesday

Advent is about the night that never stops.

Life in the northern latitudes is very much dominated by light. For about ten weeks, beyond the arctic circle the sun does not set, producing the white nights of summer. During the dark winter period the sun remains below the horizon for about seven weeks, creating the polar night, known in Finnish as *'camos'*. This perpetual darkness takes its toll on the physical and emotional health of the people. Tension, fear and crime rise. People long for the light and hate to be alone, even installing neon lights around their windows while some governments sponsor artificial sunlight rooms. That's what physical darkness can do.

But what about the darkness in people's lives this Advent? It can differ from one person to the next. It can be poverty or war, struggling with addictions, the indignities that old age or failing abilities can cast upon you. More finally, the darkness can be looking to the day when they lose a loved one through death.

John the Baptist said that Jesus is the real light, the genuine light who changes things. He is forgiveness, he is hope, he is encouragement, he is a word of love, he is an arm of strength. He is what you need to lighten your personal darkness, when there are more questions than answers.

That little child in the manger will meet you at the point of your darkness, whatever that darkness is for you. In his lightswe shall find the strength and the illumination to carry on.

Let Christ's light end your darkness this Advent.

Amen.

Week 3: Wednesday

Advent is about the hidden greeting.

By now legions of snowmen, robins, santas and, hopefully, some religious cards, will be on their annual Christmas card sentinel duty on the mantelpieces throughout the country. Lists will be checked to see if anyone was omitted, prayers will be offered that no late runner of a card from an unexpected source will plop onto the doormat.

But what do we write on our cards? An exhortation to a Merry Christmas can sound a bit ridiculous. A prayer for a peaceful or blessed Christmas may sound overly pious for some people. Most people will probably resign themselves to a Happy Christmas. Maybe they may include the new year in their greeting, especially if they have missed the deadline.

Like many things, Christmas cards are a fairly modern custom. 1843 saw the first card sent in the post. Sir Henry Cole in that year found time had crept up on him and he hadn't enough time to send his usual Christmas letter to his friends. Ever resourceful, he commissioned a set of hand-tinted greeting cards. Unfortunately, he printed too many and so he put his surplus cards on sale, and the rest, as they say, is history.

To a people more and more used to talking, rather than writing, Christmas cards can be a chore. To those who receive your card it's a compliment. Above everything else the sender could have been doing at that time, they took time out to think only of you. What greater greeting could you receive than that quiet message of care, of love, of affection?

So the greeting really is for you and for me to remember someone who needs remembering this Christmas.

Amen.

Week 3: Thursday

—

Advent is about good times and bad.

'It was the best of times, it was the worst of times.' So begins the Charles Dickens classic, *A Tale of Two Cities*.

Yet it could easily have been said of the times when Jesus was born. Judea was a vassal state of Rome. Augustus Caesar was emperor while Herod ruled ruthlessly as local king. People scrambled to make a living. Poverty was all about and sickness was common. Justice, however, was not.

To make it worse the prophets were silent, and for four hundred years the question had been, 'Where is the Messiah?'

For many it was the worst of times. For first parents with back-to-the-wall debt, not wall-to-wall carpet, sleepless nights, echoing fridges and rooms, it can seem the worst of times.

For others, life is pretty sweet right now. Family about, happiness abounding.

For others, not so good. Empty places, celebrations diminished, Christmas promising more than it delivers. The warm glow a little less bright.

For others, even life is just plain sour. How do we carry on? Perhaps somehow, somewhere, they know it will not always be so.

But we all do have reason to celebrate. Why? Well, the

Angel Gabriel gives the reason. For nothing is impossible with God. Whatever you face today, however impossible it may seem for you today, it is not impossible for God, if we but say yes. Advent is about your saying yes to God and then letting God be God for you this Advent.

Amen.

Week 3: Friday

Advent is about making room for God.

Christmas is many things, but it is certainly a time of visiting and mending what our past year of busyness has damaged, the fragile bridge that links family and friendship.

One such bridge builder visited an elderly man living on his own. She enquired if he was lonely. 'How could one be lonely when one believes in God?' was the simple astounding reply. This was a man who had not allowed his aloneness to turn to loneliness. He was someone who understood at a gut level what Emmanuel meant, *God With Us*. He had made room for God.

Is that your story as Christmas Eve peeks in at your door? Probably, then probably not. At one level we can say Christmas isn't much anyhow, just 24 hours. For the child waiting with eager anticipation, it's fun and presents. For those with the accumulated years on their back it may promise more than it delivers.

Christmas Eve this year, in a sense, has echoes of Christmas past. It's about memories good and bad but never indifferent. You see Christmas Eve is a clearance in the forest of our lives, a space to find out what really matters. A space that makes room for God on this blessed and holy night.

As the poet Máirtín Ó Díreáin said: 'Do you know,

Mary, where you'll go this year to look for shelter for this holy child, while every door is shut in his face by the hatred and pride of the human race? Deign to accept my invitation to an island in the sea and the ancient west. Bright candles will be lit in every window and turf fires kindled on the hearth. And so make room at the hearth of your home for Christ this Christmas evening.'

Light a penny candle in your window and welcome Christ home this holy night.

Amen.

Week 3: Saturday

Preparation. Advent is about preparation.

Everybody enjoys the finished product, the nicely iced cake and finished pastries, the finely served dinner, the beautifully built home, the well raised family, the sublime musical symphony. But how many enjoy the preparation, the work that went into the finished product? Very few: for the most part, we don't like the preparation work. We would rather be on a trip than pack for it, or living in a house than building it.

Life requires preparation – it's messy but it is in the preparation that we will win or lose. It has been said that all is well that begins well, or as any carpenter will tell you, it is better to measure twice and have to saw only once. Preparation far exceeds the amount of time that you are in an actual performance, but repairing takes even longer.

There is nothing wrong with our more basic Christmas preparations. Christmas trees and tinsel and angels on trees and a child's delight at the unwrapping of gifts and chocolate and toys and feasts and laughter and sparkling eyes and pensive memories – all those things that make Christmas special should not be swept away.

But the questions is, how can they move from being no more than a passing experience to being an expression of a profound reality? Our task at Christmas is not to chop down the tree of celebration – rather it is to rediscover the real cause of celebration. Namely: God is with you in your own individual wilderness. Prepare well!

Amen.

Fourth Week

Week 4: Sunday

Today is the fourth Sunday of Advent and it's about waiting no more.

The time of waiting is drawing to a close. And the question remains – Who are you looking for? And are you hearing the invitation?

The same scenario pertains now as did so many years ago. If you were a postman, exactly how many 'Marys' engaged to a 'Joseph' could there be in a small town? So, just before your brain switches off at the over-familiar words, 'The Angel Gabriel was sent by God to a town in Galilee,' think again. This is real. As real as it became for Mary giving birth, a teenage girl in a stable – probably the most dangerous experience for women of her time.

We can think of the many solid reasons that Mary could give for saying 'No' to the angel. You know them: not the right time, it's inconvenient, not the right place, too busy, too young, not the right husband/wife/family, get someone else to do it. It seems that when you want to say 'No', any excuse will do. And yet she says, 'Yes, here I am … let it be.' Her happiness was found in believing, not in external circumstances, but in a genuine invitation from God.

It is chastening to remember that, apart from shepherds and itinerant kings, everyone missed out that first

Christmas – not because of evil acts or malice. No, they missed it because they were not looking for him.

Little has changed in the last 2000 years, has it? Who are you looking for? Have you heard your own invitation this last Sunday of Advent?

Amen.

Week 4: Monday

Advent is about possibilities.

Each person is a unique moment of grace and each has potential beyond our imaginings. Each one has their unique contribution to make.

In 1808, a war-weary world anxiously watched the march of Napoleon Bonaparte. As at any time, babies were being born. Among them, the political leaders William E. Gladstone and Abraham Lincoln, poet Alfred Lord Tennyson and composer Felix Mendelssohn. Yet, people's minds were occupied with battles, not babies. Exactly 200 years on, it is clear that these babies made a far greater contribution to history than the battles!

So it is with the birth of Jesus. The Bethlehem crowds had no inkling of the greatness in their midst. Napoleon, again, summed up the admiration of the ages for Jesus Christ:

'Alexander, Caesar, Charlemagne, and I myself have founded great empires ... but Jesus alone founded his empire upon love, and to this very day, millions would die for him.

Jesus Christ was more than a man.'

Every birth is shrouded in wonder, the mystery of unknown potential lies asleep in a parent's arms. Care is taken at the naming of a child. But the name of Jesus was not left to Joseph and Mary to choose. Jesus, or Yeshua, means 'God is Salvation'. His name describes the purpose for which he came –to be the Saviour of the world.

Where is such a saviour in your life this Advent day, and where is he encouraging your unique contribution to family and community this Christmas?

Amen.

Week 4: Tuesday

Advent is about homecoming

Christmas is the homecoming Feast Day. For some it has a really physical feel, with family and friends waiting. For others home may be not where they live now, but the place where they were born and grew up.

Advent is a time when we re-affirm that Jesus Christ is on his way to re-enter our lives once again. He wishes to make his 'home' in us. Because we are so human, we need to tell, remind and show ourselves that Christ is real, and did indeed come to our earth to love and save us all. To be a human being means that the disappointments, hurts and pains of life will hit each of us some time. While we walk on this earth, and live in bodies of flesh, we can't escape that. But the message of Christmas is that God, who created the universe, loves us and cares enough about us to put on human flesh and die for us.

We celebrate for the most part in homes. For some there will be a sore spot in their heart, knowing in faith that a loved one has, in the truest sense, gone home, to be with the Lord forever.

May he take up abode in our hearts as he did in Mary's heart and this Christmas, let every heart a manger be. Amen.

Week 4: Wednesday

Advent is about adventure

Too often we view Advent as a penitential season rather than as a time to re-focus our lives. The effort to observe Advent as a 'mini-Lent', while carrying out Christmas shopping, listening to carols and joining in the optimistic mood prevailing is often jarring.

Perhaps we would do better this Advent to abandon the struggle of trying to overhaul our lives and instead focus on our relationship with God. Perhaps we need to 'do' less in order for God to 'do' more. Let's focus on what Advent *is* instead.

Advent is the season of the pilgrim God, the God who hungers for our love, the God who intrudes into human history as being born as one of us. For a people who often speak of our journey towards God, we forget that it is God who does most of the travelling. The God who is already present in the very depths of who we are draws nearer and invites us to respond. This God insists on breaking through the wasteland into the wilderness of our hearts.

God of exiles, keep calling us home. You know the yearnings of our hearts. You also know how easily we can lose our way. May this Advent season be a time of coming home to the best of who we are. May our personal home-comings influence all the earth. We walk this day with hopeful hearts, believing that your justice and compassion will bring comfort and freedom to all who are in exile. Let Advent, for each of us, be the adventure of returning home from exile to the heart of God.

Amen.

Week 4: Thursday

Advent is about Eternal Beauty.

It's interesting how someone trawling through an attic or auction can have the eye to see beauty in what another person misses. Take pictures for instance. The right light, a better frame and that old picture's beauty can be unearthed and look out to a new generation. It was there all along, of course, but very few noticed it.

So it was with a baby in a manger. This picture is very old, but it has been copied and passed on in picture, word, song and enactment from generation to generation. Maybe you have walked other paths, other ways, left the bric-a-brac of faith to a dusty recess in your mind. You need Christmas to shine out and bring beauty, purpose and meaning to your life. In making a living, let us not forget having a life and celebrating *his* life. After all, this 'picture' is our record of a special time in history that will not occur again in quite the same way.

Let us treasure this baby in a manger as the official announcement of the day that 'God so loved the world that he gave his only Son.'

May we have the eyes to glimpse, the ears to hear and the heart to experience and live out the reality that God is Emmanuel – God with us. He is the eternal beauty who comes to live among us.
Amen.

Week 4: Friday

Advent is about Christmas

Coming up to Christmas, and the nearer shopping and postal deadlines come, the question begins to form in our minds, 'What is all this for?' 'What is Christmas about?' It all depends, of course, on what you mean by Christmas. The very word conjures up pictures in the mind, each of them precious and personal.

You see, there are many kinds of Christmases. The most frequent one is the quiet Christmas, oft used in response to the eternal query: 'Well how did you get over the Christmas?' There's the Christmas of the excited first-time parents, all excitement, love and newness, anything but quiet, where you pray that the patience will outlast the batteries in the toys. Then there's the Christmas where the love has died or dimmed at least and only the silence remains, as everyone goes through the Christmas motions. The Christmas of children, with expectations always seeming to stretch beyond what the family budget can stand. We shouldn't forget the Christmas where someone is missing and missed. On the other side of the coin, there's the homecoming Christmas, with crowded airports, terminals and roads. For a moment, the pain of the inevitable January departure is forgotten.

So many hungers of the heart, but the unchanging Christmas story feeds them all. It's a celebration of truth, goodness and togetherness in a world that knows too much falseness, evil and brokenness. At times we'll wonder why we do half of the things we're at in our cards, calls, gifts and visits. But in our heart we know that it needs to be done, not so much for the recipient, but for our sake and for God's.

Amen.

Christmas and New Year

The Blessing of the Manger
on Christmas Eve

The Holy Gospel according to Luke: 2:1-8

In those days a decree went out from Caesar Augustus that the whole world should be enrolled. This was the first enrolment, when Quirinius was governor of Syria. So all went to be enrolled, each to his own town. And Joseph too went up from Galilee from the town of Nazareth to Judea, to the city of David that is called Bethlehem, because he was of the house and family of David, to be enrolled with Mary, his betrothed, who was with child. While they were there, the time came for her to have her child, and she gave birth to her first born son. She wrapped him in swaddling clothes and laid him in a manger, because there was no room for them in the inn.

Prayer and Blessing

On this Christmas Eve we pray to you,
God of every nation and people.
From the very beginning of creation
you have made manifest your love.
When our need for a Saviour was great
you sent your Son to be born of the Virgin Mary.
To our lives he brings joy and peace,
justice, mercy and love.
As we conclude this Advent journey,
we ask you, Lord, to bless this manger.
May it remind us of the humble birth of Jesus
and raise our thoughts up to him
who is God-with-us and Saviour of all,
and who lives and reigns for ever and ever.
Amen.

Christmas Day

On Christmas day the two searches – our seeking God and God seeking us – meet at Bethlehen.

The Advent journey is now over, and as you open presents from those you love, remember that the greatest present at Christmas is not a physical one, it's spiritual. In all your celebrations take this journey to Bethlehem and share the spiritual gifts of light, wonder, obedience and preparation and the joy of truth. Share them with those you are with at this moment. I pray for you at this moment.

This Christmas Day may God open your heart to love, your mind to wonder, your ears to life, and your life to the divine presence. May you experience God's peace for your troubles this Christmas Day, God's forgiveness for your guilt, God's presence for your loneliness, God's light for your path, God's guidance for your journey, God's joy for your life.

May you know this Christmas Day the hope of this blessed season, the rejoicing and celebration of the carols, the caring found under your roof, the sharing found in giving, the good news proclaimed by the angels, the anticipation and excitement of the prophets, the assurance that all wisdom is found in scripture, and the wonder of God's love found in Jesus.

May you know this Christmas Day the twinkle of bright light in your eyes, the sound of love ringing in your ears, a vision of the Saviour in your mind, the spirit of the season in your memory, the joy of the season in your life, the faith of the Christ child in your soul, and the message of the season on your lips.

May that be your benediction this Christmas Day. Amen.

New Year's Day

New Year's Day, the turning of the year, a time to look back and reflect, a time to plan ahead into the future, as we wish each other a happy and prosperous new year.

But what is a prosperous new year? By what measure does one calculate success? Robert Louis Stevenson thought that a successful person was one who had lived well, laughed often and loved much, who had gained the respect of intelligent people and the love of children, who had filled a unique niche and accomplished his or her task.

Who leaves the world better than before, whether by a perfect poem or a rescued soul.

Who never lacked appreciation of the earth's beauty or failed to express it, who looked for the best in others, and gave the best he or she had.

And so, grateful for the blessings of a year gone by, and filled with hope as a new year begins, let us pray:

Father we kneel before you, grateful in our hearts for your many gifts to us. An old year has come once more to a close. We face with confidence and hope the beginning of a New Year with all the promise that it holds, the mixture of grief and blessings which it now keeps hidden from our eyes.

Now be with us, Father, as this new year unfolds. Through our efforts and your help, deepen the measure of peace that is ours. Bind us more closely together, to each other and to you, through your great gift of love. May the blessing of the New Year be in the hearts of all the listeners. And keep us as one in mind and heart with God this day, and all the days of the year ahead.

Amen.